ANIMAL JOKES

Distributed to Schools and Libraries
in the United States by
ENCYCLOPAEDIA BRITANNICA EDUCATIONAL CORP.
310 S. Michigan Avenue
Chicago, Illinois 60604

Library of Congress Cataloging-in-Publication Data
Woodworth, Viki.
Animal jokes / Viki Woodworth.
p. cm.
Summary: A collection of jokes and riddles
featuring all kinds of animals.
ISBN 0-89565-861-5
1. Wit and humor, Juvenile. 2. Animals – Juvenile humor.
[1. Animals – Wit and humor. 2. Jokes. 3. Riddles.] I. Title.
PN6163.W66 1993   91-44916
818'.5402–dc20   CIP / AC

ANIMAL JOKES

Compiled and Illustrated by
Viki Woodworth

Annie: Why is a hippo so clumsy?
Sally: It has two left feet.

Annie: What would happen if a hippo stepped
on a baked potato?
Sally: You'd have a hip-potato-mess!

Andy: Where do sick mares go?
Lenny: To a horsepital.

What is black and white and blue all over?
A cold zebra.

What's the difference between a doughnut and a hippo?

A hippo is harder to dunk in coffee.

Ted: Why did the baby snake cry?
Fred: It lost its rattle.

Fred: Can you get fur from a crocodile?
Ted: Yes! As fur as possible.

Fred: Why don't you take my snake on your trip?
Ted: Why?
Fred: In case it rains, it's a windshield viper.

What kind of frog can jump higher than the Empire State Building?

Any frog can jump higher than the Empire State Building. Buildings can't jump.

What did the camel eat at the movies?
Camelcorn.

Why is a wild hog no fun at parties?
He's a boar.

Andy: What does a two-headed cow say?
Lenny: Moo. Moo.

Lenny: What game do little calves play?
Andy: Mooosical chairs.

Andy: Why did the cow say "oink"?
Lenny: She was learning a second language.

Why did the boy bring his skunk to school?
For "Show and Smell."

What animal wins whenever she plays cards?
The cheetah.

What does the mother sheep make to keep the baby lamb's feet warm?
Muttons.

Sarah: What do you call a *huge* sheep with lots of hair?
Jane: A woolly mammoth.

Sarah: What do sheep say when they're glad to see each other?
Jane: Baa.

Sarah: What goes "aaB, aaB, aaB"?
Jane: I don't know.
Sarah: A sheep walking backwards.

What is a lamb on a super hot day?
A wool sweat-er.

Sarah: What do sheep wear when they swim?
Jane: Baa-kinis.

Why do elephants wear green sneakers?
So they can hide in the grass.

**What time is it when an elephant sits in
a chair?**
Time to buy a new chair.

What does an elephant take to relax?
Trunkquilizers.

What do you do with a blue elephant?
Cheer her up.

Why did the elephant hate his trip to Mexico?
Because the airline sent his trunk to Spain.

Nancy: Where does an elephant sit?
Brian: Anywhere it wants!

What do you get when you cross a doll with a fish?
A dollfin.

Why did the octopus win the fight?
He was well armed.

Margaret: How will the dogfish pay for its dinner?
Chris: With its credit cod!

Nora: How do you keep a fish from smelling?
Charlotte: Hold its nose.

Charlotte: I don't like that crab!
Nora: Why?
Charlotte: She's shellfish!

What fish would make a good boxer?
The sockeye salmon.

What do you get when you cross a kitten with a skunk?
A pew mew.

Sam: What kind of tree barks?
Joe: A dogwood!

Sam: What kind of plant do dogs chase?
Joe: Cattails.

Mike: Have you seen the Catskill Mountains?
Karen: No, but I have seen them kill mice.

What does a 200-pound mouse say?
"Here kitty, kitty."

What kind of dog loves to fly?
An Airedale.

What does a panda live on?
Just the bear essentials.

What do you get when you cross a shark with a hyena?
A fish that laughs its head off.

What do you get when you cross a shark with a bowl of tapioca?
Dangerous dessert.

How did the hippo escape from the zoo when all the exits were blocked?
It went out an entrance.

1st Opossum: Want to go out tonight?
2nd Opossum: No thanks. I'll just hang around here.

What do you get when you cross a talkative parrot with an ape?
A blab-boon.

Why do rhinos sit on marshmallows?
So they don't drown in hot chocolate.

What happens when you give a Great Dane garlic?
His bark is worse than his bite.

What's green, has four legs and a trunk?
A seasick elephant.

What's green, has red spots and a trunk?
A frog with measles on vacation.

What happened when the frog parked in a "no parking" zone?
It got toad.

What is gray, fat, and has a trunk?
A hippo on vacation.

Brian: Why is the elephant sleeping with a banana peel?
Nancy: He wants to slip out of bed in the morning.

Nancy: Why does the elephant put a peanut in his trunk?
Brian: He doesn't have a glove compartment.

Nancy: How did the trainer get the rhinoceros to laugh?
Brian: She told him an elephant joke.

What do you get when you cross an elephant and a piece of paper?
A giant spitball.

Why was the mouse's letter wet?
It had postage dew.

What kind of bird is crazy?
The loon-atic.

How do you celebrate a bird's birthday?
With a bird-day party.

How do chickens pay their bills?
By chick.

What chicken lays blue eggs?
A sad one.

What do you get when you cross a duck with a hunter?
A quack shot.

What kind of exercise does a bluebird do?
Worm-ups.

What kind of dog always wins?
A wiener-dog.

Margaret: What kind of fish chase catfish?
Chris: Dogfish.

Chris: What do they call baby dogs in Ohio?
Margaret: Puppies.

What is it called when dogs kiss?
A pooch smooch.

What dog do you see after it rains?
A poodle.

What do you get if you cross a dog with a hen?
Pooched eggs.

What do rabbits use to comb their fur?
A harebrush.

What game do little bunnies play?
Hopscotch.

What do you call a rich comedian rabbit?
A funny money bunny.

What do you call a happy rabbit who falls into a vat of honey?
A sunny honey bunny.

How do bunnies travel in the city?
By rabbit transit.

What do you get when you put a hare into a raspberry bubble bath?
A berry bubbly bunny.

Karen: What kind of cereal are you feeding that cat?
Mike: Mice Krispies, of course.

Mike: What cereal are you feeding to your cat?
Karen: Shredded Tweet.

Mike: Why are you feeding that cat candy?
Karen: Because I'm tired of him being a sour puss.

When do you feed a cat birdseed?
When it's swallowed your bird.

What do you get when you cross a kitten and a donkey?
A mewl.

Which cat won the bowling contest?
The alley cat.